I Saw My Life

Michael T. Steffen

LILY POETRY REVIEW BOOKS

Library of Congress Control Number: 2025944143

Cover design and Layout: Michael McInnis

ISBN: 978-1-957755-65-6

Published by Lily Poetry Review Books
223 Winter Street
Whitman, MA 02382
lilypoetryreview.blog/

in memory David Ferry (1924-2023)

He passed the stages of his age and youth

Contents

I Saw My Life

Wishes

Through the thatched lace of a locust tree
the eyes of the stars like grass sparkle and stare
as from one mind that has been everywhere,

seen everything and found no one thing
to turn its look from. Seeded in this valley of time
where the moon is a pebble in a shallow stream

those furthest peers into our own depth burn on
and say, O no you don't, you don't disappear.
Cast for the Fish. Retreat, retreat – the Crab.

Sting. Draw arrows. Weigh this and that. But find
your reflections. Somewhere. Even way out here.

Dreamers

There was the makeshift car behind the toolshed
we kids assembled from old Model T parts
collected over the years by one of my uncles.

The essentials: a front seat and a back seat
with foam padding flowering everywhere
the worn leather had been torn and cracked.

A steering wheel duct-taped to a headless rake handle
angled under an actual tin hood with its tarnished
chrome nose ornament through a windshield

with no glass in it. Four tires tilted against
cinder blocks that gave her elevation
and odd planks of knotty lumber for a floor-bed

that helped make up the sum of missing parts
with a heavy chrome fender propped up
behind our Lizzy and another ahead of the hood.

And fenders, disproportionate fenders now
that I think of it, stacked against the abandoned toolshed.
They shone from fragments of chipped chrome

bright enough to distract the whole business
of imagining we were going somewhere.
A set of keys to nothing were tossed up in the air

and we scrambled for them for who would drive first.
Adjacent poplars caught the wind and leaned
back against us as we set out, shifting ahead.

So Much Next to Nothing

How many trips it made from home to store
or to the Saturday morning market, the basket woven
of soft reed, amber over beige –
already trying to relieve loads from plastic bags
before we were aware of the stranglehold
of polymers.
                The strength of my mother's slender
grip, knuckles through wrist, widened my eyes
when she handed it to me through the door
home from shopping, laden with canned goods,
potatoes, onions, a roast, a quart of milk.

      Its leather strap handles were riveted
to leather hasps stitched to the tight catch
of the basket's broad lip. Errand to errand
from store to home they would not let go
of the hand that would not let go of them

              as they impressed
deep purple grooves into the meat of my palm,
taut with the body's lean opposite the heft.

      Once unloaded,
back up on the coat rack contrary as rain
gear, an umbrella's crook, a hat, the basket
relented to its prong, the worker amid apparel.

Atlases

Before the Internet
in a mostly decorative corner of the living room
sentried by the one-eyed television –
an encyclopedia set stood up on the shelves above
the cupboard where dad kept liquor and atlases.

One of our differences:
the volumes of his print version of the world
were kept in virginal spines, handled
by and large for dusting.

His inheritance *from Jefferson*, building.
He was trained on dimensional blueprints
with measurements for framing and coded
indications for piping and wiring.

Which is why, I guess, he more readily
lay his views of the world across his lap
in those large floppy spiral bound maps
that page by turned page zoomed
longitude and latitude from region to road.

There was even a Great Britain A to Z
from the evenings his thoughts
were kindled to imagine me
on my study year in England
in the contoured foothills of the South Downs in Sussex
along the A27 to Lewes Road and on to the University.

If I could have told him
about a punished giant whose name was given
to the immense grasp of this pastime of his,
I could also feel anywhere I traveled
myself under the reach of his index.

The River vs. Me

I tipped a narrow scull into the river
out in its muscle, not where people waded leisurely
back upstream in the mirror of the reservoir.

If you row you know this craft needs to be kept
centered, narrow as a river reed
but this time a cramp

kicked in one calf and like that over
I went and came up breastbone-deep digging
heels into the silty bottom, struggling to

hold onto the scull – the property of
the rowing club. Because it was not mine
I couldn't afford to lose it. A therapist

I told the account to later told me I'd been
in denial of myself. A river
called Denial! I couldn't have been

more than the crossing of an 8-lane freeway
from the shore, with as many gallons
per minute driving against me.

Kayakers paddling nearby saw me. Here
they gathered around me out of nowhere
corralling me. They couldn't drop their paddles

or physically reach out any nearer.
Yet thanks to them I made it – never having
to cross a freeway without a bridge.

There were bridges over the river both ways from me
and there they would reach beyond the end of that day
one way or the other.

Both Sides Now

The look in the two eyes, green, green –
yet one saying, *Slow down approaching me.*

The scar across the bridge of the nose yields
at crest, accounting for some preservation

of innocence lingering on the readier side of my face
when I cover the opposite side with a book

standing in front of a mirror, the glare square,
with a swirled boundary of Yin and Yang persisting

as I shift the book, looking at my look, this side
then that side, seeing here the careworn singer

cricket of summer, there the burdening ant
in how one brow lifts, the other will not.

The flare of both nostrils, one declaring
*Something around here's gone sour...*the other's wing

wanting to increase its faith in burning
one more lavender candle. The shush cleft

of the upper lip hopelessly wanting to give its secret
away with a grin, the teeter-totter down

side of the mouth from a tick it's got working
out our monthly budget. All the blame

on either side of me bristles with two-day stubble
counter-patterned to keep my Gillette attentive.

Dad? Is that you? Mom? From how deep, I must
be seeing the bust from an old temple for Janus

in times that modeled inordinate hiving of
our DNA in enchanted unison under

harvest moons. Moon face. Bright eyes –
one with a sagging lid. The one cheek

less buttoned, the sharper one. Is there no truth
in the balance of your scales? – now peering,

without the book, for the wholeness of my one regard,
wanting to un-see this divide

I have so looked into this curious hour, to the open
pores. And oh wrinkles, where is that cream for you?

Radar

Each time I beam in on one in the movies
my own searching nearness dimly flickers.
Time quickens with the needle

sweeping the element in reach
where you had always been. Then one day
your look stilled in mine, just for a bleep,

and you smiled. My eyes batted.
The sea of the world turned opaque,
enveloping, swimming clear in anonymity

where, closer, closer, read and reread
back and forth like a palindrome, singularly
that flash of you pulsed and blossomed

again on the dark instrument of *Who's there?*
The slip away? The jolt and tremor? What is
everything? Seeing it come for you?

Dear Second Person

Dear *you*
I found in translation
declining French verbs in a middle-school classroom
until then unaware

he, she, it and *they*
were things apart
from the low tone whisper
eliciting the conference of myself

in the imparting of unsettling
sparks to our ground
we would not easily trust
to the tinder of out-and-out speech.

Only you know before the story's given
the long rough drafts of
my innocence and implication
in every near miss

flinging the curtains in from the window
scattering light stuff,
now and then even a lamp's heat
or vase with its putrid water.

Furniture in the room
can be righted
where you may settle back with dust
fidgeting the pattern left in a print.

Your Last Video

There's our Jo Jo, in the video she
took of herself preparing a recipe for
braised beef neck bone and seasoned turnips
only a week or so before the accident
that devastated us. For the longest time
I couldn't bring myself to watch the clip,
sorely aware that hand, pinching the salt,
busy with the knife and onion, now lay cold
in cherrywood in the Wisconsin earth.
The oaks through winter aptly wore no green.
Wind ushered cloudy skies. I'd forgotten
about it altogether. Then one day
there it was in my files, *jo jo_s julia* –
hovering out on a new PC's large screen,
her voice chirping on to my astonishment.
Stir the vinegar briskly, adding oil,
a drop or two – oops, three... Strange how cooking
draws out the intensity in her, the swallowed
husky voice, her look's aimed fire.

Why doesn't Jo Jo smile? her mom frowned.
That isn't my little girl. True to the mother
that somehow may never be consoled.

She was determined to succeed at everything,
shadow and pith, the hairbrush in her mirror
to the subtleties in settlement depositions –
vying for partnership in the firm.

Clyde her husband didn't grasp every hand
extended from the sleeves of their tailored suits.

Her driver's heavy foot was notorious.
Either you slow down, I once barked at her
from my squirming passenger seat,
or stop the damn car and let me out.

I'll walk, I told her. *Kill yourself if you want to.*
I told her that. I didn't mean it that way
of course, and how I deal with having said it
is with admiration for her persistence that could
make me say a thing because I meant it
beyond how out of line it was. Courage,
I often wonder, or restraint from offending,
which is the greater virtue? Honesty or kindness –
wholly ignoring the context of that morning
as though it were all fate for a type
of personality, all her will. And nothing to do with
the unseen ice on the road into the curve.

16

Seeing Love

Sitting on a public transit bus
behind a teenage couple – she with her head
turned and leaning away from him,
him persisting toward her, arm around her

shoulder, trying to bring her back closer –
love is at odds, as I remember it often being
when I was their age. We called it going steady
when things were all but steady going

like this bus ride rattling over bumps, into sudden
stops. Swinging in awkward turns. Anything
but the purring Audi ride past white picket fences
and their mown lawns on a summer evening

in Swampscott. The smooth sailing a lone shore sees
ghosting in the masts out there. As if before you started
dating, life was *un*steady, discontinuous,
shaky. Without the closely attached companion

and their wants leaning away from yours,
challenging bank balance, study time, rumor
with a mind of its own, uterus.
Though I don't need to know what thorn has been

clutched in the rose between the young couple
learning the suffocating squeeze of giving in,
the visible strain of holding out, how I and Thou

drift to the exchange of envies, plover and jetty mortar,
and I catch myself uttering, ah the pain
of pride and pleading, and then counter-catch myself
how worse it could be, with no waves on which
to hold fast out there, no wind in the sails.

I Saw My Life

1.

Grant me, I begin to say the prayer –
Grant me the serenity to accept –
my eyelids heavy with sand starting to bat

then I'm dreaming another waking in the rear
of dad's old Pontiac. It leans and hums
over the speed strips nearing a toll booth –
hmmm... hmmm... I jar awake and look up
seeing the mounted rangers in the window
from our family trip, when we were kids, out to
Yellowstone. There had been forest fires
I remembered another day, being asked
to think of things I had no power over –
overwhelming as wind billowing smoke,
micro and pointed as a speck of dust
lodging itself in the nose's soft nerve,
greater than myself. Beyond expecting.
It wasn't so hard for my ego to admit.
I'm not the world's most passionate guy.

2.

My city stirs in the imagination.
At Town Hall, when you go through the entrance
into the lobby, just before Reception
assembled like a ship in a dry bottle
within a sizeable glass case there sits
a model of the town. Displaying character
detailed enough, areas built in brick
painted burnt red, the newer glass in gray.
The parks glow green, ponds and the river blue,
small slopes of hills, horseshoe of baseball park.
A cemetery's speared fence and rows of headstones.

My eyes narrow peering, in the blank space,
for names inscribed on the headstones in the model.
They aren't that detailed, squinting, my illusion
bending to the miniature city like
the silent constant eye of God. The names
would gleam forth from the stones of each of us
who lay there buried, waiting for His day.

3.

How would you answer if asked your name?

Substance and flux, matter constant and changing,
the maker of visions like Pygmalion
yearning for stone, confused his metaphors
of truth, for truth itself. He'd lose perspective
sketching – drafting a subject to the point
capturing made it only more of a thing,
failing the idea of a house
at night conspicuously revealing its
interiors, a wall of windows lighted
without shades or curtains drawn, the structure's
vulnerability, its outgoingness
adrift in that dark where anything might hide
(the wakeful artist), to encroach on the secrecy
that is part of a wall's strength.

4.

I focus my eyes: between the 1600
and 1800 blocks on Vineyard Street
the town is dissected by Atlantic Avenue.
A little beyond, at Liberty Square, a grid
of streets turns 2 o'clock and angles toward
the bank on River Street, defining Medford's
town line north north-west. The architecture
noticeably shifts from the original
standards, five stories at an even height
along the natural arbor (just under it)
with stone facades in classical designs,
a section here and there maintained in red brick
by the Medford Historical Society.

The spectacle of the modern Globe Court House
looms in baroque sculpture from 1580
to 1610 Vineyard Street, east side,
with its many windows riding west to sunsets.
North and west of the dogleg at Liberty Square
the buildings crop up into low rises –
heralds of our crouching financial district.

Water the slow erosive may allow
the great steel beams of our skyscrapers
to hold in their colossal structures for
a time ensuing total inundation
of coastal metros, when the polar ice
has melted and broken into massive bergs

raising the oceans' levels, the way a handful
of ice cubes makes a tea glass brim over.

I frown: the mere idea of this
teleological advent in our industry
in the globe's vast theater. What likelihood?
What would surviving cultures in the hills

surrounding, say, Atlantic City make
of the outcroppings? Clearly not geoid
but angular, isometric. Not of nature's
sluggish piling hand but of the squaring
mind of the being (their own) of weights and measures.
*Once gods out of the fireballs in the sky
landed on earth and built their wondrous cities...*

Mr. Brown and Mr. Weiner one day
re-vogued in hides and pelts (if any furry
animals elude this present extinction)
may momentarily, gazing at New Atlantis,
be visited by sensations of neckties
and swivel leather chairs with cushioned arms.

5.

The walkers slow to close and congregate
at the street corner where the traffic stalls
and a policeman with white gloves stands in
the intersection waving through a solemn
single file of cars marked with small flags.

Is this my invitation? It comes to me
surely as others standing with me here
I'm in the presence of a funeral
procession, having (with no thought to) joined
my hands, with my removed cap in my fingers,
forehead bowed, seized by this spirit of
occasion passing through surprisingly
capable of evoking at least this gesture
of common respect, as a breath of weather
gathers heavier collars around our shoulders.

Then the hearse drives slowly
past me. Why I cannot say
I raise my hand in a simple wave of hail
and farewell to him or her
the happy soul who holds
a coin for Charon, now at rest within
this ceremony. Today they wouldn't need
excuses for not being at work on time.

No more such thing as time – a swirl of day
and then the night when everybody joins in
with you, lying down and closing their eyes.

6.

From the balcony of our duplex this morning
I watch the sculls rowing out on the river.

Through the sliding glass door
the apartment's going inside-out.
The mirrors have been taken from the anchors
and leaned against the wall extending from
the bedroom hall into the living room
joining the kitchen entrance. Jump-to's
at organizing prompt Audrey to action –
knowing my bottomless capacity
for dawdling. Why spoil today with what
can be put off until tomorrow?

A stack of folded moving blankets
behind the sofa lies in wait to mute
and safeguard the mirrors' fragile magic.

For the meanwhile they steadily render
the comings and goings of our footwear.
Recorded in their low reflection, empty
spaces are opening (unnoticed otherwise)
throughout the apartment, still with the door
of our daughter's bedroom sealed, her things untouched –
to meet the gaze's blank unfathomable
nearness for a gasp, catching myself.

7.

Noon from midnight, if time's not linear
but with earth's model, round. At best my hope
is to be ready, unfazed by the next
unforeseeable vantage of my condition.

When a heart stops. Minutes...your whole life...
For several minutes the medics worked pumping
my chest. I saw my life flash before my eyes –
stages past, stages ahead, the work, the play,
vanities all, snow sled, books, fruit and fly
into the swirl, the relief, the loss, joy with its sob...
I'd seen the face of Death, with my hand clutching
the rail of a winding staircase, eyes rolling up.
I went backwards, away from the light,
in the inexorable tunnel, and wanted to stay there
in my savory time, in my mid-twenties...
I couldn't breathe. They beat on my chest

and I somehow made it. I survived.
To practice yoga, seeking lyrical
zeros, in minutely held contortions,
after the pressure points, to edify
and release pain, in cryptic intensities –
so legibly confined. I start to get
around again, in longer passages
of measured breathing, stepping into sensible
walks around the town, back down to the office.

8.

A shadow before me rises, in smacking youth...
The thing I love about Heyward, *twenty-two
going on forever*, with his spry
dimpled belligerence: that innocence,
his ability to chop his hand clean off
and grow it back all in the same breath –
Yeah Walt to his senior, then straightening up,
straightening his face, *I mean, yes sir, Mr. Glendon* –
even Walter grinning irrevocably.

Back where young Mister Heyward calls home
the loss of a loved roominess is felt
in the immediate physical space he rents,
a one-room studio with its closet bathroom,
elbowroom at scale, shower and mirror,
the kitchenette with cupboards over sink,
dorm fridge, hood fan for hot plate, a table
where he eats, taps away at the keyboard.

*Author, authority is out.
Nobody's going to be unique again
and there's no passion that isn't pigeonholed
by legalization, mindfulness or a membership.
Now that the Capital's owned green, the planet dying
on a machine, when college loans require
graduates entering the work force to start paying
6-digit debts to make the normal dream
of buying a home and raising a family*

unthinkable to all but the sour cream,
because our eyes are strained from staring at screens
for time, sports, weather and entertainment,
clicking through Office Manager in our cubicles,
staring in theaters, at tablets, at our phones...

the radio station with *the DJ of anarchy*
playing cooler tunes from better times –
becomes his go-to breath of air.
W-R-U-G Where R U Going?

> *Hey how does it feel*
> *to be on your own...*

Take us along on one-oh-nine point three
Medford's best continuous classic rock –

> *with no direction home...*

9.

To blurriness I take my readers off,
rub my eyes, then turn them squinting back
down to a page's haze of out-of-focus
figures. Definitions year by year
recede in the space between my near world at
my nose, and a bent arm's length, to my desk,
all fuzzing out from my natural faculties –
obstacle easily enough overcome
with just a reach to put the glasses back on.

You'd rarely see one though you knew them
as Little Red knew something beyond age
had taken the place of grandma in her bed.
By then too late, already in doom's chamber,
the simple soul barters for time with language,
*What big eyes, full of blue fire, o you – Who
are you?* Presently I would be
bartering for time with Howard Naylor,
our lupine landlord. If a wolf could speak
its glower and the low growl mounting might say
something like, *All the better to see you...*

You know when the wolf has seen you, even if
the song taunted, *Who's afraid* – you scribbling
whiskers on the picture of Virginia Woolf
(Howard Naylor resembled her) – adding
pointy ears and fangs. You see the moon
and cannot help but hear the desolate cry,
howl of the native spirit and Beat poet

as though lamenting some innate predatory
nature whose signature in the genome reads
so like our best friend's. (Trevor barks to be let
back inside through the sliding glass door.)

Talk the man into me, talk me into
getting up off this couch. Tell me the sun
has come out and the snow is melting in
the picture window. Look. The envelope
left in the screen door by the landlord – still
lying on the desk... Come open it
and see how long we've got. Talk the man into me.

From Howard Naylor, Landlord...
The language of the letter, notarized,
requires that the tenants specify
14 calendar days during which time
the premises be vacated and readied
for termination of occupancy

10.

and it seems to be the thing to do, walking along
the river, restless, piqued by the cop
who's given me a warning in the park.
"Hey buddy, keep that pint in your pocket.
City ordinance. I'd have to take you in."
"Sorry officer. Thank you."

I call him *Queen Victoria*
under my breath and walk along the river
to the steep concrete stairway leading up through
obscene graffiti, poorly lit, to the parkway
bridge, with its sidewalk over the long arch
chain-linked for a view on ten-foot railing
to keep iffy walkers (rowdy adolescents)
from falling off the side. I look down.

The river's surface is carved in dark ripples
sparsely with chemical foam, a ghost
of vapor from the warmer water against
the chill in the air, a drop
more than the length of a football field.
I look up. One could still scale the railings
and throw a leg over. A half-filled sketchbook
weighs from the bag on its strap over my shoulder.

I added one candle every day
to over 600 candles. No more candles.
God, grant me the serenity...

11.

It was a dream of her. A life ago?
Where did she come from? In dreams, where one
cannot resist. Desire, dread. Everything moving
toward wonder...toward dread...

Young Heyward should know better. For his knowing
he can't resist the mature woman's house.
It sparks adventure. Heather makes him feel
atoned. At one. Though still. Though there is pleasure
lying in her arms, the afterglow
disorients him, a feeling of loss so tangible
it weighs, it pangs. Every time he swears
he'll never knock on Heather's door again. –

You again, she smiles at Eddy. *Come on in.*

At thirty-five to Eddy's twenty-two
Heather makes him feel attuned. She's his access
to attitudes and language that belong
to a fine line of adult nonchalance
capable of navigating between
hubris and innocence, rock and whirlpool.
She's mature in her casual nudity.
In one expression she can frown and smile.

12.

We keep some recoveries intact
and in working order, like the stereo
with a turntable and its knobs, the one
to turn it on and up, the one to set
the speeds. I plug it into a tube hum
and draw my index lightly just up under
the stylus head, softly for the needle
to make a muffled scratch across the natural
grooves of my finger print... When I place
the vinyl album on the turntable with
the dog and gramophone upon the label
there comes the grainy sound of the clear rim
before the music, that is already music
to my ears, a snowy crackle, friction, contact.

I set the turntable needle down to
another album's grooves at the fourth song.
The weathered voice, melodious as rain,
of Willie Nelson warbles, *All of me,*
why not take all of me... – an old Sinatra
standard, in fact written by Gerald Marks
and Seymour Simons, in 1931 –
before my father was brought into the world.
I would have been shy of invisible,
I tell myself. Yo Mike! Not even
a desire yet, a mere whisper
tottering amid daisies and dandelions,
in the illusion of the moment: eternity.
Can't you see I'm no good without you...

Her father's life before he'd met Audrey's mother
hid to be opened in a photo album
under some binders in a bureau drawer.

To this day she stores the old photo keepsake.
The times she'd take it out, in a lull on Sunday,
with her mother gone to the épicerie
or to visit with her neighbor friends,
Audrey understood the life inside that book
had been a special one for him, and yet
a past with its own silence in this life
which, in his words, he had been blessed with,
meaning her and her mother.

They came late to him
in 1966 when Audrey was just two.
Maman was a single mother working as
a secretary at a printing press.
In that same year Albert was 48.
His older age confused more than embarrassed her
next to her classmates with their younger fathers.
(*C'est ton grand-père qui t'amène?*)

With his past in days of World War II
as she and the world grew older, it was as though
he'd entered her imagination from
mythology – the golden age of cinema,
in a society of people posed
to have their pictures taken, postured, smiling,
wearing neckties in coats, dresses and hats
in black and white, for years to fade and yellow.
Bogart, Bergman, Josette Day, Jean Marais.

13.

Next door the Hanicks as though by manner keep
their voices to low murmurs. Days go by
with Audrey and me. They are part of our lives.
A faucet runs. A chair is scooted across
the kitchen's floor tiles. Forks and spoons and knives
clink softly into the drawer's molded spaces.
The drawer closes gently. The faucet runs, shuts off.

It is the habitual reticence of our neighbors.
Not to be taken for granted, proving itself
once in a blue moon, if even – twice
a year? – when something with Mr. Hanick,
Isaac, unsettles like a fault. One night
the Medford Police were called
by an anonymous walker who'd been out
keeping his insomnia company in the moonlight.

Presto out of nowhere from the dark
a shiny object nearly striking him
crashed to the sidewalk. Isaac's Cuisinart blender.
Silverware flew tinkling down onto the street.
Take that! Maddened Mr. Hanick cried out –
shaking his fist out the window. *You... You...*

A set of tea saucers came flying like frisbees
across the lawn, followed by some ghosts
of laundry, a queen-sized bedsheet, pillowcases...

We're all human, even the most demure
among us. Must build up in you.
Any of us potentially might go
insane. Quietly maybe we all are –
sanity being an outward ability
to act, to act, to act the role you're cast in

for any given situation, walk
on any ice. A pique or stubborn thought
forgoes its cue and line in all the world
that is a stage, in the on-

going comedy for those who hold
the play together, the illusionists
adept at belief, even so good at it
they comprehend the others who go off
because perhaps reality's unmasked
unbearably to them. A father losing
his job, how much denial, how much anger
that is to swim in. How much resignation

like Achilles in the mind of Zeno
chasing the tortoise. You can't resolve the riddle
of loss, or of survival, walking on
in selflessness, in space conceived by Zeno
infinite between two things because the distance
between any two things implies the intervention
of a third thing, and between that third thing
and other things infinitely more third things.

14.

You want to have some sorrow? she had asked him
(Wasn't the question: *You want to have some fun?*) –
sensing him too shy, for being younger,
to make the first move. Heather recently
had ended a relationship. She'd found
herself standing in front of an allegorical
painting in the museum, with her hand
pointing out a figure, just like that
explaining her interpretation while
young Heyward frowned to think.

They went for coffee in the museum café.
They went for lunch. They went to the cinema.

He couldn't be happier. His heart sank
silent and light blue. Heather knew he had sinned
because he believed in sin. She also knew
they were with the cosmos and its sympathies –
if not with its semiotics.
A dove's wings clattered, abandoning the window sill.
A jeweled snake slid under the house's foundation.
Heather thought it might emerge from the cellar
bearing a message from her ex, Jason Harrow –

Sssfffear, regretsss...

15.

Days have grown warmer. Time to fold the sweaters
and corduroys away. We still have till
November for a place. "I guess we could just
sleep in the park, keep everything in storage,
shower at the Y," says Audrey scrolling
through Craigslist for apartments. Where will we
be housed? Dante had thought himself to be,
in his real life to come, destined for time
in Purgatory – pages thumbed away
for James Merrill somewhere in Oklahoma.

Wouldn't it be nice…

Let nothing go. Ignore no accident.
Admit no casual failure to acknowledge
your superiority. Admit no
test of patience. Everything is at
all moments on the line.
"Step back. Back, please" –
tensed to our opponent, each and all
on-comers. "What's with you, man? And don't go
giving me that look!" The bus jostled
everybody together. "That was my foot!"
snarling – without checking himself, red-faced.

Howard Naylor with coffee spotting the lapel
of his tweed blazer, jumping off the Route 92
Bay Street bus, had narrowly
escaped a mob uprising caused, he's sure,

by no more than the polish on his shoes –
trying to save the planet by commuting,
now second-thinking his plan not to renew
his garage space and sell his Lamborghini.

If only he found out where the other man lived!

He'd know somebody to get Caliban
fired from his job. Or have his rent jacked up.
Serve him right. Ignore no indiscretion.
He snarled, "Just wait! You'll see!" up at the windows
of the bus growling back into traffic.

16.

In Howard slept the chrysalis that could
unravel a frantic moth. Let it flutter
out to circle the crazy magnetic heat
of primal hurt, he had to watch himself
in fundamental ways. He had to eat
when hungry, cool his anger, find somebody
to talk him back from the vast spaces of
his loneliness, and rest when he was tired.

Warning prepared the mind
to understand the trials of experience,
the body individual (or social) for
the advent of change and need for new direction.
Rarely, if ever, when people are benefiting
from fire will they moderate their use of it
until the village burns down. Several times over.

17.

"I'm sorry, it was in the middle of the sidewalk,"
Naylor more irked than sorry said back to
the man in the tattered coat yelling at him. –

"You kicked my coffee over! Can't you look
where you're going?"
                              Quietly people with
their eyes and thoughts were walking to and fro
on their way back to work, stopping for coffee.

On the sidewalk in front of the café
well away from the wall, where people would walk,
there lay the cup tipped over with light brown
milk coffee spilled on the concrete. Before
he'd gathered his senses, Howard found himself
entangled in the absurdity of how
the cup had been left there for his foot to kick –

the man standing a good ten yards away
beside the news kiosk.
                              "Who," asked Howard, "leaves
their coffee in the middle of the sidewalk?"

"I don't believe this guy!" the other's
voice went up with a gesture toward the sky
attracting notice.
                              "You wouldn't," Howard sought
to reason with the unreasonable man, "you wouldn't

hide a thing by dropping it in the ocean
expecting the tide to just keep it there, would you?"

The man with the complaint tilted his head
in puzzlement with a long pause, his mouth
ajar revealing gaps between his odd teeth.
And then – "You kicked my coffee over, you" –

On from the café, Naylor found a parking
ticket under the wiper of his windshield.

18.

Across town windward and as the crow flies
above the treetops over Murray Square –
the stars and stripes profiled in zephyrs, westward
sagging mildly, stiffening forth again.

The earth was turning, Howard Naylor was aware,
all sailing in this globe of light through space
which the movements of the emblematic cloth
merely suggested. Here below, all still.
People motioned themselves along the sidewalks
doubling through the storefronts, sheltered under
the unaffected trees bellied in shadow
dully green in the warm afternoon air.

You can wait for the cows to come home
early in the morning. You can leave
a number, I promise to get right back to you...
The person on the sidewalk ahead of Howard
had stalled, searching on their cell phone screen.
The answer from the center – *Which way?* – lies
360 degrees. Come on, oh geez!
Go anywhere. Don't get stuck. I don't have all day.
"Move move *move!*" he urged, gliding around them.

He tensed with caution when approaching
the little shop at 6th and Tremont where
inevitably the pigeon feeders gathered
pigeons and pigeon paint. Lowering his head

Howard cringed at being hit up for small
change and cigarettes by the less fortunate.
They stood around the shop. Their manner wasn't
always so meek, for askers. They often got
forward, even menacing. Naylor
cited them in arguments against
the welfare state and Socialism's failure
to motivate *the naturally selected.*

19.

Look, I keep getting this call. It's unidentified.
Who are you? – Howard fairly pecking
the question at his phone. *And why are you*
calling me? He clamped his free hand tightly
over his right ear. A voice broke into fragments
through waves of static as a delivery truck
getting a green light revving in low gear
bawled into the intersection before him.
Why must one be always at their beck and call?
Who are you? Howard snarled to a busy signal
as he turned from 4th Street making a b-line for
the first door, a shiny brass and glass
revolving entrance into a hotel lobby.
Hello? Hello? In his inbox file
the previous contact read *unavailable*.
Who in this day and age...his forehead ridged.

Young bodies Howard notices by glimpses
where his eyes' beams happen to be drawn
at just the tick of a clock's hand – when an open
collared blouse leans forward to his glance
at human fruit enhanced in lingerie.
It does what (he reluctantly looks away)
to him, he can only begin to describe as
molecular. Desire's foamy sweet tooth,
the dog that needs that leash, itching, whining.

Although his mind, his sentiment, even humor
have accepted the avuncular role
his life has paddled into (unless he's fooled
to jest the eternal bachelor's meditation)
there's something ignoble in the total acceptance
that his forty-something is over the hill.

Miss Nawkay, Howard's secretary, at least
has told him he wasn't. He was a young man still.

Carol was reliable about these things,
very efficient. Though she needed to learn
to take care of herself, with those deep dark
circles under her eyes. She should get more rest.

Naylor himself (she'd tell you) worked her over hours.
For which she was not paid, though compensation
had worked out between them. It wasn't the money.
Miss Nawkay's complaint was that Howard assumed her
ever at his beck and call, no matter
what time of day or night. Weekends, holidays,
every day, every hour meant potential work time.
Once an idea struck him at closing time
or two o'clock in the morning, her cellphone jingled.
It was expected of her to be there.
Beyond this demand of time, during or off hours,
Miss Nawkay's grievances compiled a list.

Generally he was impossible to get along with.
Whether on purpose or by accident

he managed a sort of physical oafishness
around her, creating mishap after mishap,
tripping her – *Oh, 'm I bad!* – breaking a heel
off her shoe, spilling food or coffee
on her, staining her clothes. She might just as well
be married and have children, for the trouble.

He was intrusive, moreover.
He'd somehow discovered a lot about her past
and liked to embarrass or belittle her
by bringing up awkward stories, from her teen loves,
bad grades in school, the stubborn episodes
that had ruined friendships and worn at family ties.
He often degraded her. He called her lazy,
loveless and sloppy. But then any attempt
she'd make at trying to adjust to these "suggestions"
only drew contrary criticisms.
Now she was acting overambitious, mothering
and too meticulous. She should back off.

20.

Howard the perfectionist insists
no dish lie in the sink. There is a reason
we have a dishwasher. The twice-a-week
(Mondays and Thursdays) domestic Maria
knows how he expects his socks, underwear
and hankies to be folded into separate
tidy little stacks inside the upper
left-hand dresser drawer. "Separate piles."

"A visible half-inch gap," she rolls her eyes
opening and closing the drawer abruptly
to make sure this movement doesn't jostle
the socks across the line into the boxers,
the hankies into the socks. "Stay put!" Maria
warns the garments. "You want to get me fired?"

21.

"Howard! Howard!" the voice called out, a woman's
in front of the convenience store where clients
going in and coming out were stalled.
Naylor's eyes looked up – down and away.

"Mister Naylor don't know me now," she said
in front of everybody. Her fingernails
were polished ice blue, chipped, holding onto
a power drink, her gym-sculpted shoulders
sloping from her sheer tank-top printed
with silhouettes of penguins.
Howard glanced at her over the expensive rims
of his designer glasses, half-mooned, beckoning
discretion among the people, as they quietly
crowded and shifted to stand them face to face.

"I'm sorry?" he shot her a fleeting puzzled look
as though – *Who're you?* sliding by her.

"He told me they were hiring," her voice trailing off
over a complaint of green liquid shaken in the bottle.
To his turns, for all her efforts, an outsider.

22.

The bows strike the chords of the four instruments,
the melody rippling through the lower voices,
the Maiden skipping unguardedly,
Death in his deep hood on the prowl...

Turning his head from the eternity
of airing on the classical music station
he says the prayer that leaves things in the air,
guiding him through three options, readily:
Grant me the first thing. Grant me serenity.
Especially in the age of 5G that takes
thirty-minute lunch breaks, minding everything
packaged in plastic to use and be done with.
Where time is money, every second counting –

being inured to everything in piecemeal,
in flashes of notice, scrolling through X, YouTube...

To go into the secondary mantras
of Courage and Wisdom, would be tedious.

Courage and Wisdom, there are your Death and Maiden.

A lilting violin descant floats above the theme...

This is how it's been praying this prayer.
Having only the time to mean the first thing,
I ask for the sang-froid to accept these things,
fortissimo music, a cut wire swallowing files,

shave nick in my bathroom mirror, the fact
I'm a few pounds overweight (greater than myself).

The first violin pulsating in sixteenth notes...

At a scent of lavender from down the street

I pray almost to wonder for the courage
to do the laundry strewn around the apartment
to fill a Friday afternoon instead.

Chorale climaxes, breaking off...dies away...

But this too: wary of second thoughts, of missing
opportunities, I pray for the first thing.

The cello carries the theme...

23.

So where were the insiders? It's hard to tell.
They are so in, you only think you see them
here, or here. A good photographer
with some persistence may be asked to shoot them,
maybe one here, one here, a group of them
for a group portrait. No matter how
invisible insiders like to keep,
they love a token of themselves, to be
brought to mind. Especially when one
doesn't have to be there *to be there.*

Last year our companies made a net profit
well exceeding any prior year.
Streamlining healthcare should up the pulse.
Cutting contributions for Public Radio
is paving the chalkboard for future generations.
And expanding carbon extraction, we can look
forward to a thriving disaster relief market.
Call *that* a win-win, gentlemen...

                                       Howard Naylor's

fingers stroked his angular shaven chin
over the tight dark crimson knot of his silk tie,
frozen his expression, his nature's, at any pretense
on behalf of his CEO of confidence.

The man now belonged to universal
principles, such as the ones expressed
in far-reaching equations, Good and Evil,

$E=MC^2$, the latter being
preferred for giving him an integral role.

Orders, the man refined his purpose further,
stagnate without neogenesis from chaos.
Not that orders – powers in themselves –
avoid corruption, without scrutiny.

I scratch your back, you look the other way.
And so it goes, doors open of themselves,
another foot slips in. To your hung chin
there is this: Grow up. Get a life. It happens.
Naylor grinned, listening. He frowned.

Good news smelled of sophistry and sycophancy.
Production charts had dramatically leveled off
that slow first quarter of the fiscal year –
while still at a sizeable profit: NO GROWTH!
And every member at the board meeting knew
this stuck like a thorn in Naylor's paw.
His mane bristled. His barbed tail flickered
regally side to side. His silence roared.

Advances in – the CEO continued –
advances in "intelligent" technologies
will soon enable Dradco to downsize
even more staff. They're even developing programs
capable of evaluating employee
productivity, as well as applicant credentials.
Human Resources will soon be fully automated.

24.

Eddy Heyward looks left, looks to his right.
The office is empty. They have gone to lunch.
Quickly, with blood pulsing in his forehead,
Eddy's fingers race over the keyboard
to the computer at his desk. A window
appears on the PC (*property of
The Medford Daily Mirror*) opening
a database of files, as who does not dream
of mellifluous lines in code?
                                        He finds
the link to additional services, requiring
permission and a password. Heyward traces
the IP address, locates the FTP site
containing the uploads for *Stereo*, the WP font
desired for the logo of his blog.

A sensation of thrill, as on a rollercoaster's
brink to the plummet, sifts through his stomach,
his head lightly spinning. He has bypassed
the password protection by hacking into the server
where the web address is registered –

when from the far end corner of the office
from the bathroom – the door swings open...

The pulse beats in Eddy's temple vein,
his face flushing deep red, bending his look
down at a document beside the keyboard.

And I walk by him, making as if oblivious.

Doesn't even work here, Eddy thinks.
Couldn't have noticed anything. Just walked by.

I ask the intern, "Going for lunch?"
not stopping at his desk but strolling by,
and Eddy thinks, *Just walking by like that...*

Or had the illustrator purposefully kept his head
from looking down at him, on purpose kept
his look up toward the door, as though to say
Oh no, not noticing you as you pirate
protected files from the Mirror database...

Shshsh, Eddy exhales silently. *He saw me.*

25.

You have your phone to look at, to appear
preoccupied and unavailable –
employed, eyes to yourself, not dangerous –
not just to stand there. Where do I put my hands? –
Looking lost. *Reply* Facebook prompts.
Hit MENU, APPS, to GAMES, catch a shark,
race through a labyrinth – with others
gathering at the bus stop. If they get
a glimpse of your screen they'll think you're a dinkhead.

Eddy scrolls to APPS, opening X, newsfeeds,
politicians, entertainment, weather...
What genre or language will Hermes use to get
his message through, to tell you what you need
to hear today, now that it's understood
strangers don't talk with one another?

I can't believe the illustrator caught me
red-handed... Not that he'd have to tell...

Then wouldn't you know it here she comes
arm in arm and all in harmony,
three legs between, a sack race, Heather Campbell
with Mister jaw and dimples, Jason Harrow.
They're back together.
Here you are.

They were strolling toward the harbor. Simple Eddy
counting the cracks along the sidewalk. He looked up
and there they were blindingly, in his face –
so in his face, he had to second-guess
if they were there at all. And what about
this smile-frown of Heather's – *Hey-ya Eddy!*
(*You wanna have some sorrow?* she had asked him
once upon a time, when this was...*real*...their story...)
Harrow's expression walks a thin line,
nearly Hallmark, between sympathy
(furrowed brow) and self-defense (clenched jaw).

This should have been enough, this one encounter.

26.

The air feels heavy. Clouds castle in the sky.
Everything resists reckoning.
The nearly empty rooms on Hudson Street
make his knees feel weak.

The men arrived and took the furniture
out of the living room, leaving the space
an emptiness of eggshell,
                              of abandoned
walls with their reach up to the lofty ceiling.

They'd taped up curtains of translucent plastic,
themselves becoming shadows with the tools
that tapped and scraped. A power sander whined.

A powder of old surfaces was kept
from the adjacent kitchen as it fell
and drifted onto the plastic, onto the paper
taped on the hardwood floors as I imagined
a soul being emptied of its residues –
the hollowing of this life, yes, yet also
the renovation of a dwelling where
we're somehow welcomed back. I had a dream
of grandpa Elgin sitting in his chair
by the old cathedral radio, a journal
across his lap. He turned its quiet pages.
Then the startling knock on the door...
The tall walls echoed, *Well, look who's come for a visit.*

27.

What do you do when you have seen the dead?
I googled near death on the Internet
and located a definition: the state
of physical detriment at which a person
would be expected to die. At forty-something
obviously no more in the crisp salad
days, I could this day, sciatica nagging
in ham, stake my claim to physical detriment –
certain as ever – unless they do come up
with an immortality pill – to die. One day.
Which may just be the point: that for all of us –
this life we live, with coughs, boarding planes,
counts as a near death experience, crossing a street,
to whatever degree we're aware of it.

28.

Now you garden in the mountains
in a valley under a giant, Mount Evans,
in hiking distance of the reaches of Lake Echo.
Fragrant, repellant
lavender and loosestrife guard the perimeters.
Near the house inside a wire fence
on account of – *You wouldn't believe the deer out here –*
your vegetables: beans, potatoes, milk turnips,
sunflowers, summer squash. Mornings must
remind you of the miracle of life
on earth that so imbues us as to make us
oblivious to light and air as we grow
lunar with spite for the burdens of our bodies
and the personalities of others around us.
At one time you were thinking of moving to
Antarctica, to continue your research
on that land of vast ice,
earth's nearest analog to space.

Lake of placidity, oak of resolve,
grown up, the psychology selection
questionnaires and isolation labs
weeded you in, one of two out of ten
out of a thousand would-be's,
a fifth of whom, you wondered,
filtered themselves out by answering
Yes to Do you smoke? Pages and pages
Of What would you do if questions:
...if one of the crew members started making

sexual advances at you? ...if a coworker
on a spacewalk should perish? You looked straight
at me, remembering these questions, saying,
"Same answer for both: *Cut them loose.*"
I chuckled at how obvious this must be,
Love and Death haunting humans even in space.

You said an astronaut considers it
an honor, as the sailor at sea,
to be buried in the element of their vocation.

29.

One's only daughter goes off to
a university, getting the grant
dad swallowed his shallow pride for.

He hardly foresaw how it was going to hit him
watching her glide up the escalator
past Security, to her terminal
at the airport that afternoon.
Doesn't every dad watch his daughter do this?

If only a father wouldn't make such a big deal
of being left behind. You would never
tell her that. Cara had things to do
with her life, far beyond
whatever dad's hard swallow could see.

30.

The chair she sat in had the left-wing window.
Its compressed view held her attention
with a curious intensity
she would recall years later as prophetic
on her first spacewalk doing simulation
work on a satellite, as she looked down,
pillowed in darkness, at the lighted blue
earth, her home, in its bridal veil of clouds.

This day she watched the runway from the window.
It sped and narrowed then swung out of view,
the plane's hull gently rolling skyward
then leveling back for a strained look down at
the wonder of abundance in the arbor
cradling the houses of the neighborhoods –
reaching down in her handbag for a book
of poetry by Elizabeth Bishop.

31.

I make sense of these photographs of her.
Here she's eleven; here she's twenty-five.
In a summer dress; helmet, oxygen mask.
Weaving a daisy chain; whizzing at mock speed.
Vulnerable; inviolable.
A butterfly; an irrefutable theorem.

My doctor slides a camera tube inside me.
My daughter glides into the ghost light of the stars
also to take these photographs
of the cosmos of me
I could never otherwise embrace.

She's in the Air Force now, I tell myself.
Why not?

32.

When she left for the academy
I declared my carefreedom
and rode on Greyhounds, getting glimpses of
rural America, the small towns and farms,
cattle and crops afield, the eyesore
weather-tilted barn in faded red
and close enough to the highway to show some sign
in whipped white paint, advertising a hardware store
or truck stop *5 mi.* I got off the bus
and stayed in Pittsburgh for a couple months
sleeping in a park, showering and eating
at a nearby Salvation Army, working
from a labor pool a few days a week
for spending money. I helped move people's furniture,
unloaded trucks, demoed out old houses
and buildings for remodeling... When it rained
I sometimes sat up through the night in one
of the airport terminals with stranded travelers
whose layover time, or cost, prevented them
from getting a hotel room. Speaking of which –
I soon learned the waste of hotel rooms.
There were better things to spend my money on.
Movies, music downloads, butter mints...
In my sleeping bag on starry nights, sometimes
camping with another or other wanderers
I fell asleep listening to their stories,
listening to the cars go by.

33.

A look up at the night sky finds the angled
triad of Orion lining for the Bull,
beyond the bellied sail of Orpheus' harp,
the Pleiades marveling in their unearthly
theater. Only to close
my eyes and feel the wind's tug over the river
deriving from no other media
somehow turning this discouragement, the void beyond,
around. It was you, Cara,
the stargazer, oddly taking up
interest for a field trip to the planetarium,
who pointed the constellations out
to me anew. After so many
years, how could I ever
find my way out from under them?

34.

We take our last walk around the neighborhood
this evening. The houses' lighted windows
argue by turn transparency and blinds,
the family at table no look violates
through bivouacs of potted vines to purely
decorative wall paper, flash (ice blue)
of a big screen succumbing to commercials.
Our separate living rooms these days do not
commonly laugh at the same joke, unless
cosmically at that great joke on us all
and on the stars above: to each its own
irrevocably. It's what the person's said
emphatically drawing their curtain against us.

35.

I could've taken her over my knee
for scaring me like that. I'd woken up
in the wee hours. Trevor had been scratching
restless on his cushion beside the bed,
a low moan in his yawn. *Let's warm some milk.*
The thought ran through my mind. *Warm milk.* It wasn't
going to let me go back to sleep.

Then – *What in the?* – my head still in the lighted
refrigerator door, I heard the dog's
tags jingle. Funny Trevor hadn't
even barked. It was Cara's voice, *Hey boy,
hey Trevor, good dog! Hey pops!* Looking at me
standing in my running shorts, holding the half
full carton of milk. She glided softly
across the darkened kitchen floor and tucked
her head into my left shoulder.
                              "I thought you were at school."
"I came home for the weekend."

36.

What kind of bird it is... A quick bright yellow
undertone of breast plumage with a
brown collar, no mistaking for a finch.
It was a sound first, a sudden
sharp dull thud (sharp for the swiftness, dull
feathery) – *ffffpltt* – intercepted by
the picture window giving out onto the patio.

Now there it lies beside a shift crack in
the patio concrete, as though to magnify
this tragedy of a held breath: it isn't moving,
fragile creature. Audrey thinks *too late*
going into the kitchen for a paper towel
to roll it up and undertake the mortal remains
sanitarily to dispose of in one of
the grass bags by the curb awaiting pickup.

But when she reaches down for it with her shadow
over the unscanned animal, it makes
a quiver, hopping to its little feet –
darting back into the sky, as though never.

37.

How does one steel oneself? –
I wondered, bending
into a fetal crouch on the empty floor.
Odd how a place
holding so much of the past, holds onto you presently.
And I wept.

That November evening we carried the remaining boxes
from the apartment at 16 Hudson Street
loading them on the truck for the last trip
to Joseph Street. The whole next day flashed by
in the hollow rooms, swabbing the floors and walls,
spackling chips and holes from hooks we'd hung
the mirrors and pictures on. We took the curtains
and the Venetian blinds down from the windows,
these last guardians of a privacy
where Audrey and I had welcomed a child
to grow with her, reweaving our common lives.

The last bones of gossamer had been swept from
the corners of the ceilings. At the door
to be drawn closed and locked this one last time
I paused to look around the empty rooms
as though – when Audrey reached and hit the light
drawing me out into the early
darkness of autumn, against the speckled night.

The keys dropped in, the mailbox lid made a clink
familiarly. Something had been delivered.

38.

I'm not the world's most passionate guy.
I walked back by the old house where we'd mulled
around the blocks and thought, often with my Ipod
listening to Patti Smith, on Hudson Street.
I'd stood at the crosswalks here waiting for the changing light,

forgetting the newspaper.

39.

The squares and streets were wreathed
in red ribbons and lighted up for Christmas.
Afternoons Audrey would take you wrapped up
warm in your little winter scarf and cap,
your nose scarlet and runny, in the stroller
out for a breath, the sidewalks here and there
from recent snow in banks that breathed their chill
against the vaporous warmth of blue sunlight.

You dropped spare change in the kettle by the bell
for the Salvation Army, scanned the thrift shop,
went to the park. Mom set you in
the swing, your little mittens clutching the chains
as she gently pushed. *Weee,* you both sang...

She had watched the mothers with their children...
She'd had no luck herself with bread. It wouldn't rise.
You hadn't come to live with us for good
until you were already 12.
And no, never even my astronaut in the stars.
I made that up too. I have no luck with bread.

40.

Audrey, dear partner of my nightmares,
she never pushed you in a swing
except in imagination. Then it was ever
the last push from where you, our adopted daughter,
spreading your arms, flew off into the sky –
growing smaller and smaller in the endless ether
into a near voice – *Mom!* – waking her.

The little girl was born in 1984
in Canny-Barville, in upper Normandy
on the west coast of France. She was the daughter
of a French Minister and his mistress,
a British professor whom my wife researched for.

But Audrey Morvant wasn't my wife yet.
There we were on a train in 1994.
It was summertime. People were heading
to the celebration of the 50th anniversary
of D-Day, the amphibious invasion
carried out by the Allies to liberate
Nazi-occupied France. I was going there
in homage of a great uncle.
                              The little girl,
Cara Durnais, sat by the pretty French woman.
The girl had earbuds listening to a Walkman.
The woman was reading a book. Every now and then
she'd look out through the window of the train.
She'd look across the aisle between the rows

of seats in the filled carriage. Our eyes met.
Audrey's first words to me: *Ce n'est pas ma fille.*
She leaned to put her arm around the girl.
I work for her mother. But If I ever had a daughter...

41.

Cara joined cross-country in her freshman year
in high school, stud in her navel,
hair blue, fluorescent... By then you were on
your third stay with us, having enough
experience with your real mother's relapses
using heroin, to be convinced your home
would now forever be away from home
with Audrey and me. It was only now
you called us, shyly at first, "mom" and "pops"
ever diverting your eyes approaching us
with a spaced hug. It was your undeniable
curse and gift from addiction: to be elusive
but also resilient.
      With the dozen other
young women your age up through 18, you
trained through September's heat and March's
ice, with pulled groins, calf cramps, turned ankles,
gasping with stitches in your side, catching
last-leg second winds, through rain and sleet,
uphill, uphill, over the valley and through
the woods, hooded in your scarlet sweatshirt.

You'd learned, while your body was being sculpted
and unsexed for this dark blossom of your age,
to crave the hardship of a daily run –
how this could help you spend your rage, and feed it.

But then you keep running.

A Softly Spoken Man

who drank with my father
and had served in Korea

one night led a platoon out
onto a field when

                 a staccato
barrage of gunfire

                 sounds
flew at them

         lifting overhead

in dark silhouettes of startled pheasants.

Poultry

I never knew how Sunday could last.
I mistook the Cornish hen
with aromatic garlic and rosemary
for resistance

where crusts from risen dough were useful.

That we would be sitting
at the table till evening fell,
how could this half past noon begin to know?

Once in a lifetime at least
difference could be pronounced
between let-down and the unexpected

with generous stings of mustard
to wipe from my nostril
                                        – as little
by little appetite
gestured at tender strands of breast
and kept our silverware busy.

Omaha

Laid out in a quiet sprawling cross
over trimmed grass, attended by
shorn conifers and fanned oaks,
the rows of headstones enchanted
this silence striking

its palpable paradoxes,
      the stunned and abiding serenity
      commemorating the earth-shattering rage
         of war,

         the neat depersonalized monumentalism
      drawing in so intimately
      shifting one's inner posture
      to short-breathed goodness
      as when visiting a church or hospital –

turning a door's corner into
a vast ward of 9,388
mothers in childbirth all in one day.
Only no cries of labor, no birth cries.

This was the memorial of the dead. Their cry –
with the low thrum of the tide on the beach below.

The living dropped on parachutes nearby,
more than a thousand veterans, on June 6,
1994, a half century
after the battle of Normandy, D-Day.

Most of these paratroopers
were over 70 now, not quite the men
they had once been. Earl Draper's main chute
failed to open. He ended up
in a marsh with an injured back. Others broke
an arm, a leg...

President Clinton gave a speech
that broke each of their hearts. *You saved the world.*

Shoulders that had staunchly carried
their body's weights in gear
now frail under
fifty more years of graced life
and a breath of emotion
shook uncontrollably, weeping.

Age-carved faces
that had grimaced defiance under the hail
of gunfire and roar of bombshells
in this soft sunlight of acknowledgment and thanks
lowered, sniffing, shedding irrepressible tears.

I'd explain it
to the parents of my English language students
in on the joke –
Not your Omaha...
That I'd been raised near Omaha, Nebraska.

Alone, bordered in a dormitory room
with a coffee maker and a toaster oven,
I was pitied and invited
for weekends at their tables
set with more food than this poem has lines for,
cider, Bordeaux, Calvados.

And out for the winding ride
along the Channel cliffs
to the beach near Coleville-sur-mer,
this other Omaha. You could stand outside
the American Cemetery's entrance
and look down on the weekenders
in their bathing suits, the sun umbrellas
and spread towels, the dog chasing the frisbee

then turn in the other way to mull around
the stretching rows of clean white Lasa marble headstones,
most of them in Latin crosses. My initial
visit there I was drawn to
a stillness never known. As if I alone
had happened on it. Though I was sharing this
with countless others around me there and then,
before and after.

It was pure resonance. Humming. Mute.
A thought so thought, I couldn't come to words for it –
the hush and void of the sky off the cliffs
absorbing the calm blue of the sea

so utterly changed from the gray day
in newsreels with soldiers spilling from Higgins ramps,

the difference held in the one place
between this luminous present
and its glorious tragic past
rife with irony
that could fold a smile to a frown,
turn a frown to a grin, weighing

to bend and gnarl the apple groves
all along the base

of the bluffs
                    to the horizon.

Back When: Four Generations

My great grandmother
Loulou Taggart
way back in 19-oh-something
more than a hundred
years ago, in eternity,
on the front porch
of their farm in western
Nebraska, in a rocking chair
sat holding her son
Erwin, 18 months old
and already eternal
for being with her
that afternoon at the wash house.
When her back
was turned, he tipped an open
bottle of lye to his lips
and swallowed.

For or despite the pleat
above her upper lip
it was told the angels sang to her
all that night
as she sat rocking Erwin
gazing out through prisms
at the star-clustered sky
over the edge of the prairie.

She kept
her sanity to raise two daughters

one of whose daughters
is my mother who told me
the story
and we loved great grandma's
slab bacon for breakfast

when we went to visit them
up to my 14th birthday.
That's not bad, four generations
under one roof
eating breakfast together as the stars
were shepherded home.

For his good- and light-heartedness
my great grandfather
only understood he would
never understand
the intensity from that day
of his wife's pale blue eyes
when she would look up
at a migrating V of geese
or over at the stable
when one of the horses whinnied.

He knew in their courting days
his eyes had held
a similar look for her, for her only.

Though she stayed bound
to her duty

ongoing with the farm and family,
she could cast that look
almost of condemnation
which is the look
of hopeless devotion
anywhere.

Back When: Bayeux

weft of when
right to a realm
brought boats with men and horses to a wary
welcome, to widen English vocabulary

with curious culture
home to hearing
the still air for the woods' warblers, its hushes…
So pricketh hem Nature in hir corages

wrested in origins.

Our word-horde was woven
first in this interference,
in artistry
memorably embroidered,
deeply our being's signposts from forgotten
feats and symbols, captioned in vestigial Latin
showing a time, its people, standing in awe
(ISTI MIRANT STELLA) of something in the stars.

You my guide good
at deciphering signs,
auspicious birds
and heraldic beasts
to explain the unseen

playfully needled also to please,
Aesop's fox with the crow's dropped cheese,

Aelfgyva in her veil,

Turold wither-high holding the horses...

Skywalk

A pheasant's flight over a country road
came to mind once when I was in the city
tubed in the glass of a skywalk

looking down at the traffic on the street
on the way from one building's wide throughways
past pricey boutiques to a Starbucks and ATMs.

Under gray rain, if you knew your way
through the construction labyrinth of downtown,
you didn't need to open an umbrella.

Mine kept furled neatly in my hand.
My head was full of everything going
into work, with this one suspended glimpse

of the world around me thickening in a drum
of downpour, then hushing at the let-up,
the dark wet street below eye-beamed

with headlights, glowing with tail lights.
Night had fallen clear on my way home.
I had a minute to stop and hover

imagining myself sole in ascent
through a hazy nimbus of the buildings' lights
up into an utter blind gap of space

where the charts of the stars clustered
to a stunned emptying of the mind before

I came down with my nothing among the commuters.

Acknowledgments

My warm thanks to the editors of the following journals for publishing poems included in this collection:

Ibbetson Street — "Wishes"

Poetry on the Path — "Omaha", an excerpt as a broadside

The Poetry Porch — "Four Generations"

spoKe — "Dreamers"; "So Much Next to Nothing"; "Atlases"; and "The River vs. Me"

Synchronized Chaos — "Both Sides Now"; "Radar"; "Your Last Video"; "Skywalk"

About the Author

Michael Todd Steffen lives in Somerville, Massachusetts. He helps coordinate The Hastings Room Reading Series, and frequently publishes articles about new and established poets on the Boston Area Small Press and Poetry Scene website. His own poems have appeared in journals, including *The Boston Globe, The Dark Horse, Everse Radio, North of Oxford* and *Ibbetson Street*. Boris Dralyuk (managing editor for *Nimrod Journal*) writes, *I have read [Steffen's] poems with enormous satisfaction. His lines are supple and wear their unmistakable wisdom lightly.* Calling his second book, *On Earth As It Is*, "important work," Joan Houlihan noted Steffen's *intimate portraits, sense of history, surprising wit and the play of dark and light...the striking combination of the everyday and the transcendent.*